muffin magic

muffin magic

RYLAND
PETERS
& SMALL

LONDON NEW YORK

Senior Designer Sonya Nathoo
Senior Editor Céline Hughes
Production Controller Maria Petalidou
Art Director Leslie Harrington
Publishing Director Alison Starling

First published in the US in 2010
by Ryland Peters & Small
519 Broadway, 5th Floor
New York, NY 10012
www.rylandpeters.com

The recipes in this book have been published
previously by Ryland Peters & Small.

10 9 8 7 6 5 4 3 2 1

Text © Fiona Beckett, Tamsin Burnett-Hall,
Maxine Clark, Linda Collister, Tonia George,
Brian Glover, Nicola Graimes, Rachael Anne
Hill, Louise Pickford, Fran Warde, Laura
Washburn, Lindy Wildsmith, and Ryland
Peters & Small 2010

Design and photographs
© Ryland Peters & Small 2010

ISBN: 978 1 84975 031 8

Library of Congress Cataloging-in-
Publication Data

Muffin magic.
    p. cm.
Includes index.
ISBN 978-1-84975-031-8
I. Beckett, Fiona.
TX770.M83M825 2010
641.8'157--dc22
                        2010008238
Printed in China

Notes
• All spoon measurements are level unless
otherwise specified.
• Ovens should be preheated to the
specified temperatures. Recipes in this book
were tested using a regular oven. If using a
convection oven, follow the manufacturer's
instructions for adjusting temperatures.
• All eggs are medium, unless otherwise
specified.

Recipe credits:
Fiona Beckett
Bacon, onion, & cheddar mini-muffins

Tamsin Burnett-Hall
Blueberry & apple muffins
Cornbread muffins

Maxine Clark
Warm chocolate muffins

Linda Collister
Chorizo & cheese muffins
Christmas mini-muffins
Cornmeal, bacon, & herb muffins
Double chocolate mini-muffins
Gingerbread mini-muffins
Lemon, almond, & blueberry muffins
Maple bran muffins
Marmalade muffins
Oat & peach muffins
Pecan, orange, & cranberry muffins

Tonia George
Berry crumble muffins
Chocolate chip & peanut butter muffins
Dairy-free banana, date, & bran muffins
Sugary jam donut muffins

Brian Glover
Zucchini, cheese, & herb muffins

Nicola Graimes
Carrot & walnut muffins

Rachael Anne Hill
Dried apricot muffins

Louise Pickford
Pecan & chocolate muffins
Warm blueberry & almond muffins

Fran Warde
Oat & apple muffins
Spelt berry muffins
Spiced muffins
Whole-wheat banana & chocolate muffins

Laura Washburn
Apple spice muffins
Pear & chocolate muffins

Lindy Wildsmith
Triple chocolate chip muffins

Photography credits:
Caroline Arber, pages 1, 21, 32

Martin Brigdale, pages 31, 57, endpapers

Peter Cassidy, pages 3, 5 centre, 6, 7, 8,
20, 26, 33, 44, 46, 51, 54, 60, 63

Nicki Dowey, page 17

Tara Fisher, pages 15, 24, 40, 61

Jonathan Gregson, pages 2, 5 above, 9,
16, 18, 28, 41, 48

Richard Jung, pages 12, 30, 37

Diana Miller, page 14

William Reavell, pages 39, 42, 49, 55,
56, 59

Debi Treloar, page 36

Ian Wallace, pages 5 below, 35, 38

Philip Webb, pages 13, 22-23, 25, 29, 50

Kate Whitaker, page 10

Polly Wreford, pages 34, 53

contents

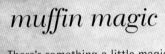

muffin magic

There's something a little magical about throwing together a few basic ingredients, spooning the mixture into paper cases, and then watching in awe as scrumptious muffins bake and rise in the oven. No matter how many times you've watched it happen, it'll always seem as though some kind of alchemy has taken place. And what's especially exciting is that muffins can range from virtuous and sustaining, to indulgent and wicked. So whatever mood you're in, you'll find a recipe here that fits the bill.

breakfast

spelt berry muffins

Spelt is an ancient variety of wheat known to be favored by the gluten-intolerant as it is easier to digest. Its flour adds texture to these muffins and makes them an easy and healthy muffin to start the day.

1⅔ cups spelt flour

2 teaspoons baking powder

½ teaspoon baking soda

½ cup sugar

2 eggs, beaten

6 tablespoons vegetable oil

1 cup frozen berries of your choice (no need to thaw)

a 6-cup muffin pan, lined with paper cases

Makes 6

Preheat the oven to 350°F.

Put the flour, baking powder, baking soda, and sugar in a bowl and mix well. In a separate bowl, beat together the eggs and oil. Pour into the dry ingredients, then add the berries. Mix together quickly—do not beat or overmix otherwise the muffins will be tough and dry.

Spoon the mixture into the paper cases and bake in the preheated oven for 30–40 minutes, or until a knife inserted in the middle comes out clean.

maple bran muffins

1 cup sour cream

½ cup whole milk

⅔ cup wheat bran

⅓ cup wheat germ

1 large egg, beaten

4 tablespoons maple syrup

1 cup all-purpose flour

1 teaspoon baking powder

½ teaspoon baking soda

a pinch of salt

1 cup shelled pecans, chopped

a little coarse sugar,
for sprinkling

*a 12-cup muffin pan,
lined with paper cases*

Makes 12

Sour cream is the key to fine-tasting, rich, and moist bran muffins. They taste even better if you let the bran mixture soak for a while before it's baked, as suggested in the recipe.

Combine the sour cream with the milk in a large bowl, then stir in the wheat bran and wheat germ and let soak for 30 minutes.

Meanwhile, preheat the oven to 350°F.

Stir the egg and maple syrup into the sour cream mixture. Sift the flour, baking powder, baking soda, and salt onto the mixture. Mix together quickly—do not beat or overmix otherwise the muffins will be tough and dry. Stir in the pecans.

Spoon the mixture into the paper cases and sprinkle each muffin with a little sugar. Bake in the preheated oven for about 25 minutes, or until firm to the touch. Can be frozen for up to 1 month.

lemon, almond, & blueberry muffins

Everyone loves a blueberry muffin but these are particularly energizing as they include lemon peel and juice, and freshly ground almonds.

⅓ cup whole blanched almonds

1¾ cups all-purpose flour

1 tablespoon baking powder

⅓ cup sugar

grated peel of 1 unwaxed lemon

1 large egg

1¼ cups milk

2 teaspoons freshly squeezed lemon juice

4 tablespoons vegetable oil

1 cup fresh or frozen blueberries (no need to thaw)

a 12-cup muffin pan, well greased

Makes 12

Preheat the oven to 400°F.

Put the almonds in a food processor or blender and grind to a coarse meal. They should have more texture than commercially ground almonds. Transfer to a large bowl and sift in the flour and baking powder, then mix in the sugar and lemon peel.

In a separate bowl, lightly beat the egg with the milk, lemon juice, and oil. Pour into the dry ingredients and stir just enough to make a coarse, lumpy mixture. Add the blueberries and mix quickly—do not beat or overmix otherwise the muffins will be tough and dry.

Spoon the mixture into the prepared muffin pan, filling each cup about two-thirds full. Bake in the preheated oven for about 20–25 minutes, until golden and firm to the touch. Can be frozen for up to 1 month.

dairy-free banana, date, & bran muffins

These muffins are full of fiber and super filling. As with all muffins, stir them only briefly, as this rocky batter gives them their characteristically clumpy, rough texture.

1 cup plus 2 tablespoons whole-wheat flour

⅔ cup plus 2 tablespoons wheat bran

a pinch of salt

2 teaspoons ground cinnamon

2 teaspoons baking powder

2 eggs

⅓ cup honey

¾ cup soy milk

⅓ cup vegetable oil

1 cup pitted dates, chopped

3 bananas, sliced

a 12-cup muffin pan, lined with paper cases

Makes 10–12

Preheat the oven to 350°F.

Sift the flour, ⅔ cup of the wheat bran, the salt, cinnamon, and baking powder into a large mixing bowl.

In a separate bowl, beat the eggs with the honey, soy milk, and oil. Pour into the dry ingredients and scatter the dates and bananas on top. Using a large spoon, fold until the mixture is moistened—do not beat or overmix otherwise the muffins will be tough and dry.

Spoon the mixture into the paper cases until they are two-thirds full and scatter over the reserved bran. Bake in the preheated oven for 18–22 minutes.

blueberry & apple muffins

To increase your intake of vitamins, minerals, fiber, and energy-giving calories, eat these muffins with one or two pieces of fresh fruit and you'll be set for the day.

1⅓ cups whole-wheat flour

1½ teaspoons baking powder

½ teaspoon salt

½ teaspoon ground cinnamon

½ cup old-fashioned rolled oats

1 cup fresh or frozen blueberries (no need to thaw)

1 eating apple, peeled, cored, and diced

1 cup plain yogurt

1 egg, beaten

6 tablespoons honey

3 tablespoons safflower oil

½ teaspoon baking soda

a 12-cup muffin pan, well greased

Preheat the oven to 375°F.

Sift the flour, baking powder, salt, and cinnamon into a mixing bowl, tipping in any bran left in the sieve. Reserve 2 tablespoons of the oats for the top of the muffins, then stir the remainder into the flour, followed by the blueberries and apple.

In a separate bowl, whisk the yogurt, egg, honey, and oil together. Mix in the baking soda, then immediately pour into the dry ingredients. Mix together quickly—do not beat or overmix otherwise the muffins will be tough and dry.

Spoon the mixture into the prepared muffin pan and scatter the reserved oats on top. Bake in the preheated oven for 20 minutes, or until the muffins are risen and golden. Can be frozen for up to 1 month.

Makes 12

dried apricot muffins

*If, when it comes to choosing between breakfast or
an extra five minutes in bed, you choose the extra five
minutes, this is the breakfast for you. Simply grab a
muffin from an airtight container as you head out of the
door and you have a healthy, filling breakfast that can
be eaten on the move.*

¾ cup dried apricots, chopped

1 cup unsweetened muesli

2 cups self-rising flour

1 teaspoon baking powder

1 cup unsweetened apple juice

3 tablespoons vegetable oil

⅓ cup honey

1 large egg

*a 12-cup muffin pan,
lined with paper cases*

Makes 12

Preheat the oven to 375°F.

Put the apricots, muesli, flour, and baking powder in a large
mixing bowl and stir. In a separate bowl, mix the apple juice,
oil, honey, and egg. Fold into the dry ingredients—do not beat
or overmix otherwise the muffins will be tough and dry.

Spoon the mixture into the paper cases. Bake in the preheated
oven for 20 minutes, or until golden and risen.

berry crumble muffins

2¾ cups all-purpose flour

3 teaspoons baking powder

1 teaspoon baking soda

¾ cup sugar

½ teaspoon salt

2 eggs, beaten

1 stick unsalted butter, melted

¾ cup sour cream

¼ cup whole milk

1¼ cups raspberries

Topping

¾ cup all-purpose flour

5 tablespoons unsalted butter, chilled and cubed

2 tablespoons sugar

3 tablespoons slivered almonds

a 12-cup muffin pan, lined with paper cases

Makes 12

These look like the muffins that are sold in cafés and that seem to have exploded out of their pans with their generous proportions. There is no secret trick to this— just fill the paper cases up to the top.

Preheat the oven to 325°F. Grease the surface of the muffin pan where the muffins will rise and stick.

To make the topping, put the flour and butter in a food processor and pulse briefly, just until the butter is blended. Tip out into a bowl and add the sugar and almonds, pressing the mixture together with your hands.

To make the muffins, sift the flour, baking powder, baking soda, sugar, and salt into a large mixing bowl. Put the eggs in a small bowl, add the melted butter, sour cream, and milk and whisk to combine. Pour into the dry ingredients and scatter the raspberries on top. Using a large spoon, fold until the mixture is moistened—do not beat or overmix otherwise the muffins will be tough and dry.

Spoon the mixture into the paper cases right to the top. Finish by scattering over the topping. Bake in the preheated oven for 25–28 minutes.

oat & apple muffins

Children love helping to make these muffins, and they certainly enjoy eating them. With the benefits of oats and apples and the lack of butter, these muffins are a nice compromise on a sweet treat first thing in the morning.

½ cup old-fashioned rolled oats

1½ cups all-purpose flour

2 teaspoons baking powder

½ teaspoon baking soda

½ cup sugar, plus extra
for sprinkling

2 eggs, beaten

6 tablespoons vegetable oil

2 eating apples, peeled, cored,
and grated

*a 6-cup muffin pan,
well greased*

Makes 6

Preheat the oven to 350°F.

Put the oats, flour, baking powder, baking soda, and sugar in a bowl and mix well. In a separate bowl, beat together the eggs and oil and pour into the mixing bowl. Add the grated apple and mix together briefly—do not beat or overmix otherwise the muffins will be tough and dry.

Spoon the mixture into the prepared muffin pan. Sprinkle the top of each with a little extra sugar and bake in the preheated oven for 30–40 minutes, or until a knife inserted in the middle comes out clean.

1 cup all-purpose flour

1 cup whole-wheat flour

1 tablespoon baking powder

⅓ cup sugar

⅓ cup shelled pecans, chopped

grated peel of ½ orange

1 large egg

1¼ cups milk

2 teaspoons freshly squeezed orange juice

4 tablespoons vegetable oil

1 cup fresh or frozen cranberries (no need to thaw)

a 12-cup muffin pan,
well greased

Makes 12

pecan, orange, &
cranberry muffins

*Pecan, orange, and cranberries are a winning
combination. The great thing about these tasty muffins
is that you can use either fresh cranberries in season, or
dig out that bag of frozen cranberries that you've been
saving up for a baking afternoon.*

Preheat the oven to 425°F.

Sift the flours and baking powder into a large bowl, then stir
in the sugar, pecans, and orange peel. In a separate bowl, lightly
beat the egg with the milk, orange juice, and oil. Pour into the
dry ingredients, stirring quickly with a wooden spoon until just
mixed. Add the cranberries and stir briefly, using as few strokes
as possible. Do not beat or overmix otherwise the muffins will
be tough and dry.

Spoon the mixture into the prepared muffin pan, filling each
cup about two-thirds full. Bake in the preheated oven for about
20 minutes, or until golden brown and firm to the touch. Can
be frozen for up to 1 month.

oat & peach muffins

What makes these muffins special is the fresh peaches, so try to make them in summer when peaches are at their tastiest. Eat the muffins warm by themselves, or with a fruit salad compote and plenty of plain yogurt.

1⅓ cups old-fashioned rolled oats

1⅓ cups buttermilk

1 large egg, lightly beaten

6 tablespoons vegetable oil

½ cup plus 1 tablespoon light brown sugar

1½ cups all-purpose flour

1 teaspoon baking powder

½ teaspoon baking soda

½ teaspoon ground cinnamon

¼ teaspoon grated nutmeg

2 almost-ripe peaches, pitted and flesh cut into large chunks

a 12-cup muffin pan, well greased

Makes 12

Preheat the oven to 425°F.

Put the oats and buttermilk in a large bowl and let soak for 10 minutes. Add the egg, oil, and sugar and mix well.

Sift the flour, baking powder, baking soda, and spices onto the soaked oat mixture and stir briefly. Quickly fold in the chopped peaches. Do not beat or overmix otherwise the muffins will be tough and dry.

Spoon the mixture into the prepared muffin pan, filling each cup about two-thirds full. Bake in the preheated oven for about 20–25 minutes, until golden brown and firm to the touch. Can be frozen for up to 1 month.

apple spice muffins

A virtuous mix of apples, raisins, whole-wheat flour, buttermilk, and loads of warm spices, these muffins are perfect for breakfast, but also good in lunchboxes.

1 cup all-purpose flour

⅓ cup whole-wheat flour

1 cup packed dark brown sugar

1 teaspoon baking soda

¼ teaspoon baking powder

1 teaspoon ground cinnamon

½ teaspoon each ground nutmeg, ginger, and cloves

a pinch of salt

1 cup buttermilk

½ cup vegetable oil

1 teaspoon pure vanilla extract

1 tart apple, such as Granny Smith or Jonagold, peeled, cored, and finely chopped

2 oz. raisins or golden raisins

Frosting

2 x 8-oz. packs cream cheese

1 stick unsalted butter, softened

1 cup confectioners' sugar

1 teaspoon pure vanilla extract

a 12-cup muffin pan, lined with paper cases

Makes 12

For the frosting, put the cream cheese, butter, sugar, and vanilla in a bowl and beat with a handheld electric whisk until smooth. Refrigerate until needed.

Preheat the oven to 350°F.

In a mixing bowl, combine the all-purpose flour, whole-wheat flour, sugar, baking soda, baking powder, cinnamon, nutmeg, ginger, cloves, and salt. Mix well to combine.

In a separate bowl, combine the buttermilk, oil, and vanilla. Pour into the dry ingredients, folding in with a spatula to blend thoroughly. Add the apple and raisins and mix just to combine—do not beat or overmix otherwise the muffins will be tough and dry.

Spoon the mixture into the paper cases, filling each almost to the top. Bake in the preheated oven until puffed and a skewer inserted in the center of a muffin comes out clean, about 25–35 minutes. Transfer to a wire rack, let cool completely, then spread the top of each muffin with frosting before serving.

marmalade muffins

Seville orange marmalade makes a gorgeous baked treat. These are simple, no-fuss muffins, perfect for baking in a large batch and freezing. Warm them up in the oven for a tasty breakfast bake.

1 cup all-purpose flour

1 cup whole-wheat flour

1 tablespoon baking powder

a large pinch of salt

1 large egg, lightly beaten

1¼ cups milk

2 teaspoons freshly squeezed orange juice

4 tablespoons vegetable oil

⅔ cup thick-cut Seville orange marmalade

a 12-cup muffin pan, well greased

Makes 12

Preheat the oven to 425°F.

Sift the dry ingredients into a large bowl, mix thoroughly, then make a well in the center. Add the egg, milk, orange juice, and oil. Stir the marmalade to break up any large clumps, then add to the bowl. Mix quickly to form a coarse, slightly streaky batter —do not beat or overmix otherwise the muffins will be tough and dry.

Spoon the mixture into the prepared muffin pan, filling each cup about two-thirds full. Bake in the preheated oven for 20 minutes, or until lightly browned and firm to the touch. Can be frozen for up to 1 month.

popular favorites

triple chocolate chip muffins

Everyone loves chocolate muffins! This recipe includes chocolate spread, which will make it particularly appealing to children.

1⅔ cups self-rising flour

2 teaspoons baking powder

2 tablespoons cocoa powder

¾ cup sugar

3½ oz. good-quality bittersweet chocolate, chopped

1 egg, beaten

4 tablespoons chocolate and hazelnut spread

6 tablespoons vegetable oil

⅔ cup milk

a 12-cup muffin pan, lined with paper cases

Makes 12

Preheat the oven to 400°F.

Sift the flour, baking powder, and cocoa powder into a mixing bowl, then add the sugar, chocolate, egg, chocolate and hazelnut spread, and oil and mix well with a wooden spoon. Add the milk a little at a time, stirring well between each addition, until the mixture has a good pouring consistency.

Spoon the mixture into the paper cases and bake in the preheated oven for 20–25 minutes, or until the muffins are well risen and firm to the touch.

Variation Substitute the chocolate and hazelnut spread with 4 tablespoons of freshly made espresso coffee and the chocolate with 1 cup chopped walnuts. Add an extra ¼ cup sugar and an extra egg to the mixture.

whole-wheat banana & chocolate muffins

The chocolate and whole-wheat flour make this a muffin that combines indulgence with virtue. It's also great for using up those overripe bananas in the fruit bowl.

1⅔ cups whole-wheat flour

2 teaspoons baking powder

½ cup sugar

½ cup bittersweet or milk chocolate chips (or chop up 2½ oz. chocolate)

2 eggs, beaten

6 tablespoons vegetable oil

2 bananas

a 6-cup muffin pan, lined with paper cases

Makes 6

Preheat the oven to 350°F.

Put the flour, baking powder, sugar, and chocolate chips in a bowl and mix well. In a separate bowl, beat together the eggs and oil. Pour into the dry ingredients. Mash the bananas with the back of a fork, add to the bowl, and mix together quickly—do not beat or overmix otherwise the muffins will be tough and dry.

Spoon the mixture into the paper cases and bake in the preheated oven for 40 minutes, or until a knife inserted in the middle comes out clean.

pecan & chocolate muffins

The secret to making these muffins perfect is to use good bittersweet chocolate, chopped, which gives a better flavor and texture than storebought chocolate chips.

¾ cup shelled pecans, plus extra, chopped, to decorate

1½ cups self-rising flour

1 teaspoon baking powder

⅔ cup packed light brown sugar

1 egg

4 tablespoons maple syrup

1 cup milk

4 tablespoons unsalted butter, melted

3½ oz. good-quality bittersweet chocolate, finely chopped

a 12-cup muffin pan, lined with paper cases

Makes 12

Preheat the oven to 400°F.

Put the pecans in a food processor and whiz until finely ground.

Sift the flour and baking powder into a bowl and stir in the ground pecans and sugar. In a separate bowl, beat the egg, maple syrup, milk, and melted butter. Pour into the dry ingredients and mix, then fold in the chocolate.

Spoon the mixture into the paper cases and sprinkle the chopped pecans over the top. Bake in the preheated oven for 18–20 minutes, until risen and golden.

spiced muffins

These easy-to-make muffins are packed with aromatic spices. Chopped apple and bananas help to keep them deliciously moist while lashings of maple syrup add a smoky, sticky sweetness.

1⅔ cups self-rising flour, sifted

¾ cup plus 2 tablespoons packed light brown sugar

¼ teaspoon ground cinnamon

¼ teaspoon grated nutmeg

½ cup milk

1 egg, lightly beaten

3 tablespoons peanut oil

1 eating apple, peeled, cored, and finely chopped

2 bananas, chopped

10 teaspoons maple syrup

a 12-cup muffin pan, lined with 10 paper cases

Makes 10

Preheat the oven to 350°F.

Mix the flour, sugar, cinnamon, and nutmeg in a large bowl, then make a well in the center. In a separate bowl, mix the milk, egg, and oil. Pour into the well you have made in the dry ingredients. Stir quickly with a wooden spoon until mixed—do not beat or overmix otherwise the muffins will be tough and dry. Fold in the chopped apple and bananas.

Spoon the mixture into the paper cases until they are two-thirds full. Make a hollow in the top of the muffins with the back of a teaspoon and add 1 teaspoon maple syrup to each one—don't worry if it drizzles out. Bake in the preheated oven for 20 minutes.

chocolate chip & peanut butter muffins

You can't really go wrong with salty peanuts and sweet chocolate. If you love Reese's Pieces, then this is the muffin you've been waiting for.

2 cups all-purpose flour

2 teaspoons baking powder

½ teaspoon baking soda

⅓ cup sugar

1 cup crunchy peanut butter

1 large egg, beaten

4 tablespoons unsalted butter, melted

½ cup plain yogurt

⅓ cup whole milk

⅔ cup milk chocolate chips

a 12-cup muffin pan, lined with paper cases

Makes 12

Preheat the oven to 350°F.

Sift the flour, baking powder, and baking soda into a large mixing bowl, then add the sugar and peanut butter.

In a separate bowl, combine the egg, melted butter, yogurt, and milk until well mixed, then stir in the chocolate chips. Pour into the dry ingredients. Using a large spoon, fold until the mixture is moistened—do not beat or overmix otherwise the muffins will be tough and dry.

Spoon the mixture into the paper cases until they are two-thirds full. Bake in the preheated oven for 20–22 minutes, until golden and well risen.

warm blueberry
& almond muffins

More indulgent than the Lemon, Almond, & Blueberry Muffins on page 12, these are best enjoyed warm from the oven, perhaps when friends come round for tea.

1¾ cups all-purpose flour

1½ teaspoons baking powder

1 teaspoon apple pie spice

½ cup ground almonds

¾ cup sugar

1 egg

1¼ cups buttermilk

4 tablespoons unsalted butter, melted

2 cups fresh or frozen blueberries (no need to thaw)

2 tablespoons shelled almonds, chopped

a 12-cup muffin pan, lined with 10 paper cases

Makes 10

Preheat the oven to 400°F.

Sift the flour, baking powder, and apple pie spice into a mixing bowl and stir in the ground almonds and sugar.

In a separate bowl, combine the egg, buttermilk, and melted butter until well mixed. Fold in using a large spoon—do not beat or overmix otherwise the muffins will be tough and dry. Fold in the blueberries.

Spoon the mixture into the paper cases until they are three-quarters full. Scatter with the chopped almonds and bake in the preheated oven for about 18–20 minutes, until risen and golden. Remove from the oven, let cool slightly on a wire rack, then serve warm.

sugary jam donut muffins

This is the muffin equivalent to a warm, sugary jam donut, but without the deep frying. Of course the muffins are more cakey but they are just as delicious.

2 cups plus 2 tablespoons
self-rising flour

½ teaspoon baking soda

a pinch of salt

¾ cup sugar

⅓ cup safflower oil

⅔ cup plain yogurt

½ teaspoon pure vanilla extract

2 large eggs, beaten

⅓ cup blueberry jam

2 tablespoons unsalted butter,
melted

*a 6-cup muffin pan,
lined with paper cases*

Makes 6

Preheat the oven to 375°F.

Mix together the flour, baking soda, salt, and ½ cup of the sugar in a large mixing bowl.

In a separate bowl, combine the oil, yogurt, vanilla, and eggs and beat together. Pour into the dry ingredients and swiftly mix together, until just combined—do not beat or overmix otherwise the muffins will be tough and dry.

Drop 1 heaping tablespoon of the batter in each paper case. Make a dip in the mixture and spoon in a heaping teaspoon of the jam. Divide the remaining batter between the paper cases to cover the jam. Bake in the preheated oven for 18–20 minutes, until well risen. Set aside, still in the pan, to cool for 5 minutes.

Brush the tops of the muffins with the melted butter and roll in the remaining ¼ cup of sugar.

carrot & walnut muffins

2½ cups all-purpose flour

1½ teaspoons apple pie spice

1 tablespoon baking powder

¾ cup packed light brown sugar

8 oz. carrots, peeled and grated

½ cup shelled walnuts, chopped

9 tablespoons unsalted butter, melted

2 large eggs, lightly beaten

5-6 tablespoons milk

12 walnut halves, to decorate

Topping

¼ cup cream cheese

2 tablespoons unsalted butter, softened

3 tablespoons confectioners' sugar

½ teaspoon pure vanilla extract

a 12-cup muffin pan, lined with paper cases

Makes 12

Carrot and walnut cake—but in an irresistible, individual portion. These look slightly more elegant than other muffins, so they wouldn't look out of place at an afternoon tea party or coffee morning.

Preheat the oven to 400°F.

Sift the flour, apple pie spice, and baking powder into a large mixing bowl. Stir in the sugar, carrots, and chopped walnuts.

Pour the melted butter into the flour mixture with the eggs and milk and mix gently—do not beat or overmix otherwise the muffins will be tough and dry.

Spoon the mixture into the paper cases, then bake in the preheated oven for 20 minutes, or until risen and golden. Transfer to a wire rack to cool.

To make the topping, beat together the cream cheese, butter, confectioners' sugar, and vanilla until smooth and creamy. Spread the cream cheese mixture on top of the muffins, then decorate each with a walnut half.

savory

bacon, onion, & cheddar mini-muffins

1 tablespoon safflower oil

2½ oz. cubed pancetta or bacon

1 small onion, finely chopped

1 heaping tablespoon plain yogurt

about ¼ cup milk

1 cup plus 2 tablespoons all-purpose flour

1½ teaspoons baking powder

¼ teaspoon salt

2 tablespoons grated Parmesan

1 large egg, lightly beaten

3 tablespoons unsalted butter, melted

⅓ cup coarsely grated cheddar

a 12-cup mini-muffin pan, lined with mini-muffin cases

Makes 12

You might like to make these delicious mini-muffins for a picnic. They're reminiscent of a cooked breakfast but not only are they less greasy and calorie-laden, they're also bite-sized, perfect for when you're on the go.

Preheat the oven to 375°F.

Heat the oil in a small skillet and fry the pancetta for a couple of minutes until it starts to brown. Add the onion, stir, and cook over low to medium heat for another 5 minutes until the onion is soft, then set aside to cool.

Put the yogurt in a measuring cup and mix in enough milk to bring it to just over the ⅓ cup mark. Sift the flour into a bowl with the baking powder and salt. Add the Parmesan and make a well in the center. Pour the egg, melted butter, and yogurt and milk into the flour and mix in quickly—do not beat or overmix otherwise the muffins will be tough and dry. Fold in the bacon and onion.

Spoon the mixture into the mini-muffin cases and sprinkle each with cheddar. Bake in the preheated oven for 20–25 minutes, or until fully risen and well browned.

2 tablespoons olive oil

6 oz. small zucchini, topped, tailed, and sliced or finely diced

2 scallions, thinly sliced

1 red chile, seeded and finely chopped

1½ teaspoons chopped thyme, plus 18 small sprigs

1¼ cups all-purpose flour

⅓ cup fine yellow cornmeal

2 teaspoons baking powder

½ teaspoon baking soda

1 teaspoon sugar

1 cup grated Parmesan

½ teaspoon paprika

1 large egg, beaten with ⅔ cup sour cream and ¼ cup milk

4 tablespoons vegetable oil

5 oz. firm goat cheese or feta cheese, diced

sea salt and freshly ground black pepper

an 18-cup muffin pan, lined with paper cases

Makes 18

zucchini, cheese, & herb muffins

These tasty muffins are just right for a lazy brunch or as an accompaniment to a bowl of soup. They are best eaten freshly made and still warm, but can be reheated for a few minutes in a low oven.

Preheat the oven to 400°F.

Heat the olive oil in a small skillet over medium heat, then add the zucchini, scallions, and chile. Add a pinch of salt and cook very gently for 3–4 minutes until the zucchini have lost their raw look, but still retain a crispness. They should not brown. Stir in the chopped thyme and let cool.

Sift the flour, cornmeal, baking powder, baking soda, and sugar into a bowl and stir in ¾ teaspoon salt, a little black pepper, two-thirds of the Parmesan, and the paprika. Rapidly mix the beaten egg mixture and the vegetable oil into the dry ingredients—do not beat or overmix otherwise the muffins will be tough and dry. Stir in the zucchini mixture and the goat cheese.

Spoon the mixture into the paper cases. Sprinkle each muffin with the remaining Parmesan and top with a thyme sprig. Bake in the preheated oven for 20–25 minutes—they should just spring back to a light touch.

cornbread muffins

Cornbread is a popular traditional recipe. This flavored version is made as muffins that can be served with a bowlful of soup or a slow-cooked casserole. They're very quick to make and you can use fresh or frozen corn.

1½ cups self-rising whole-wheat flour, preferably stoneground

1 tablespoon baking powder

½ teaspoon sea salt

¾ cup cornmeal or polenta

1 teaspoon cumin seeds

½ – 1 red chile, seeded and finely chopped

2 tablespoons freshly chopped cilantro leaves

½ cup fresh or frozen corn kernels

1⅓ cups skim milk

1 egg, beaten

3 tablespoons safflower oil

freshly ground black pepper

a 12-cup muffin pan, well greased

Makes 12

Preheat the oven to 375°F.

Sift the flour, baking powder, and salt into a mixing bowl, tipping in any bran left in the sieve. Add a grinding of black pepper, then stir in the cornmeal, cumin seeds, chile, cilantro, and corn.

In a separate bowl, mix the milk, egg, and oil together, then pour into the dry ingredients and stir together quickly—do not beat or overmix otherwise the muffins will be tough and dry.

Spoon the mixture into the prepared muffin pan. Bake in the preheated oven for about 20 minutes, or until risen, firm, and lightly browned.

cornmeal, bacon, & herb muffins

These savory treats are delicious with light, buttery scrambled eggs or omelets, cold ham, and tomatoes. Make them with any fresh herbs you have to hand.

4 slices of bacon, diced

1 cup plus 2 tablespoons cornmeal or polenta

1 cup all-purpose flour, sifted

¼ teaspoon freshly ground black pepper or hot red pepper flakes

1 tablespoon baking powder

2 large eggs, lightly beaten

1 cup milk

1 tablespoon bacon fat (see recipe), or vegetable or safflower oil

1 teaspoon maple syrup

1 tablespoon freshly chopped herbs, such as chives or parsley, or sliced scallions

a 12-cup muffin pan, well greased

Makes 12

Preheat the oven to 425°F.

Put the bacon into a cold skillet, nonstick if possible, and fry until golden and crisp. Remove the bacon and transfer to a plate lined with a paper towel. Drain off all but 1 tablespoon of the fat in the skillet (if necessary, make up to this amount with vegetable or safflower oil).

Put all the dry ingredients in a large bowl and mix. Add the bacon, eggs, milk, bacon fat or oil, maple syrup, and herbs. Mix quickly to make a coarse, slightly streaky batter—do not beat or overmix otherwise the muffins will be tough and dry.

Spoon the mixture into the prepared muffin pan, filling each cup about two-thirds full. Bake in the preheated oven for about 15 minutes, or until lightly golden and just firm to the touch. Can be frozen for up to 1 month.

chorizo & cheese muffins

4 cups all-purpose flour

2 teaspoons baking powder

a pinch of salt

freshly ground black pepper

8 oz. Swiss cheese, diced

4 oz. thickly sliced chorizo sausage (or ham, or fresh or frozen corn kernels), diced

2 large eggs, beaten

7 tablespoons unsalted butter, melted

1½ cups whole milk

a 12-cup muffin pan, lined with paper cases

Makes 12

Good for parties and picnics, as well as children's lunchboxes, these muffins are filled with molten cheese and spicy Spanish sausage.

Preheat the oven to 400°F.

Sift the flour, baking powder, and salt into a large bowl, then add a few grinds of pepper, the cheese, and chorizo. Make a well in the center of the mixture.

Pour the eggs, butter, and milk into the well in the mixture in the mixing bowl. Mix quickly to make a coarse batter—do not beat or overmix otherwise the muffins will be tough and dry.

Spoon the mixture into the paper cases and bake in the preheated oven for 30 minutes, or until golden brown.

special occasions

double chocolate mini-muffins

For parties and after-dinner treats, small, one-bite muffins are always popular. These can be left plain, or dusted with confectioners' sugar, nuts, or chocolate chips.

½ stick unsalted butter, softened

¼ cup sugar

1 large egg, beaten

½ cup sour cream

⅓ cup white, bittersweet, or milk chocolate chips, plus extra to decorate

1 cup all-purpose flour

¼ cup cocoa powder

½ teaspoon baking powder

½ teaspoon baking soda

a pinch of salt

confectioners' sugar, to dust

mini-muffin pans, lined with about 30 mini-muffin cases

Makes about 30

Preheat the oven to 350°F.

Put the butter and sugar in a mixing bowl and beat with a wooden spoon until fluffy. Beat in the egg until thoroughly combined. Finally, beat in the sour cream followed by the chocolate chips.

Sift the flour, cocoa, baking powder, baking soda, and salt into the bowl and mix quickly—do not beat or overmix otherwise the muffins will be tough and dry.

Spoon the mixture into the mini-muffin cases, then decorate with a few extra chocolate chips. Bake in the preheated oven for about 12–15 minutes until firm to the touch. Let cool on a wire rack and serve dusted with confectioners' sugar.

christmas mini-muffins

Not as sweet as some muffins, these are good for brunch along with a cup of coffee during the festive weekend when fresh (or frozen cranberries) are around. They also make a thoughtful gift for a friend.

1¼ cups all-purpose flour

1 teaspoon baking powder

a pinch of salt

¼ cup sugar

grated peel of ½ orange

½ cup chopped pecans,
plus 2 tablespoons to decorate

1½ tablespoons raisins

½ cup fresh or frozen
cranberries (no need to thaw)

1 large egg, beaten

4 tablespoons unsalted butter,
melted

⅓ cup milk

confectioners' sugar, to dust

*mini-muffin pans, lined with
about 30 mini-muffin cases*

Makes about 30

Preheat the oven to 350°F.

Sift the flour, baking powder, and salt into a mixing bowl.
Stir in the sugar, orange peel, chopped pecans, and raisins.

Put the cranberries into the bowl of a food processor and chop
roughly. Stir into the flour mixture.

Combine the egg with the melted butter and milk and stir into
the flour mixture with a wooden spoon.

Spoon the mixture into the mini-muffin cases, then decorate
with the extra pecans. Bake in the preheated oven for about
12–15 minutes until barely golden and firm to the touch. Let
cool on a wire rack and serve dusted with confectioners' sugar.

gingerbread mini-muffins

7 tablespoons unsalted butter

2 tablespoons molasses

2 tablespoons honey

⅔ cup packed dark brown sugar

½ cup milk

1¼ cups all-purpose flour

1 teaspoon baking soda

1 tablespoon ground ginger

1 teaspoon ground cinnamon

a good pinch of salt

1 large egg, beaten

2 oz. stem ginger, drained and finely chopped

royal or glacé icing, or icing pens, to decorate

mini-muffin pans, lined with about 36 mini-muffin cases

Makes about 36

Spicy, sticky, and mouthwatering, these mini-muffins are popular with children. Get them to decorate them with icing pens and give them as gifts to their friends.

Preheat the oven to 350°F.

Put the butter, molasses, honey, sugar, and milk in a saucepan over low heat and melt gently. Remove from the heat and let cool for a couple of minutes.

Meanwhile, sift the flour, baking soda, ground ginger, cinnamon, and salt into a mixing bowl. Pour in the cooled, melted mixture, then the egg. Mix thoroughly with a wooden spoon. Mix in the stem ginger.

Spoon the mixture into the mini-muffin cases. Bake in the preheated oven for 15 minutes, or until firm to the touch. Let cool on a wire rack, then decorate with icing.

warm chocolate muffins

Make these divine, super-chocolatey muffins to eat straight out of the oven while the chocolate is still soft and melting—they're so irresistible that there won't be any left by the end of the day!

2 cups plus 2 tablespoons all-purpose flour

3 tablespoons cocoa powder

2½ teaspoons baking powder

½ teaspoon baking soda

6 oz. bittersweet chocolate, roughly chopped

3½ oz. milk chocolate, grated

2 large eggs, beaten

½ cup packed light brown sugar

1¼ cups sour cream

7 tablespoons unsalted butter, melted

a 12-cup muffin pan, lined with paper cases

Makes 12

Preheat the oven to 400°F.

Sift the flour, cocoa, baking powder, and baking soda into a large bowl and stir in the chopped and grated chocolates.

In a separate bowl, beat together the eggs, sugar, sour cream, and melted butter. Pour into the dry ingredients and stir until just combined and the mixture is fairly stiff—do not beat or overmix otherwise the muffins will be tough and dry.

Spoon the mixture into the paper cases and bake in the preheated oven for 20 minutes, or until risen and firm. Leave in the pan for about 15 minutes before turning out onto a wire rack. Serve warm.

pear & chocolate muffins

3½ oz. bittersweet chocolate, roughly chopped

7 tablespoons unsalted butter

1 cup sugar

7 oz. cream cheese

2 eggs

1½ cups all-purpose flour

1½ teaspoons baking powder

1 teaspoon ground cinnamon

a pinch of salt

14 oz. ripe pears (about 2–3), such as Williams, peeled, cored, and diced

3½ oz. bittersweet chocolate chips

a 12-cup muffin pan, lined with paper cases

Makes 12

Pears have the ability to partner chocolate possibly better than any other fruit. In this recipe they snuggle up to lots of bittersweet chocolate and tangy cream cheese, and some cinnamon adds a pleasing spiciness.

Preheat the oven to 375°F.

Put the chocolate and butter in a heatproof bowl and set it over a large saucepan of simmering water—do not let the bottom of the bowl touch the water. Stir gently as it melts. Remove the bowl from the heat just before it has melted completely and allow it to finish melting in the residual heat. Set aside.

Combine the sugar and cream cheese in a mixing bowl. Beat with a handheld electric whisk until well blended. Add the eggs and melted chocolate mixture and beat until well blended.

Combine all the dry ingredients in a separate bowl and mix well. Tip into the chocolate mixture and, with the whisk on low, mix until just blended. Fold in the pears and chocolate chips.

Spoon the mixture into the paper cases and bake in the preheated oven until a skewer inserted in the center of a muffin comes out almost clean, about 20–30 minutes.

index

conversion chart

Measuring butter:
A US stick of butter weighs
4 oz. which is approximately
115 g or 8 level tablespoons.

Volume equivalents:

American	Metric	Imperial
1 teaspoon	5 ml	
1 tablespoon	15 ml	
¼ cup	60 ml	2 fl oz.
⅓ cup	75 ml	2½ fl oz.
½ cup	125 ml	4 fl oz.
⅔ cup	150 ml	5 fl oz. (¼ pint)
¾ cup	175 ml	6 fl oz.
1 cup	250 ml	8 fl oz.

Weight equivalents:

Imperial	Metric
1 oz.	30 g
2 oz.	55 g
3 oz.	85 g
4 oz.	115 g
6 oz.	175 g
8 oz. (½ lb)	225 g
9 oz.	250 g
10 oz.	280 g
12 oz.	350 g
13 oz.	375 g
14 oz.	400 g
15 oz.	425 g
16 oz. (1 lb)	450 g

Oven temperatures:

170°C	(325°F)	Gas 3
180°C	(350°F)	Gas 4
190°C	(375°F)	Gas 5
200°C	(400°F)	Gas 6
220°C	(425°F)	Gas 7